Cambridge Plain Texts

HOOKER

PREFACE TO THE LAWS OF ECCLESIASTICAL POLITY

T0346151

HOOKER

PREFACE TO THE LAWS OF ECCLESIASTICAL POLITY

CAMBRIDGE
AT THE UNIVERSITY PRESS
1922

CAMBRIDGE UNIVERSITY PRESS
Cambridge, New York, Melbourne, Madrid, Cape Town,
Singapore, São Paulo, Delhi, Mexico City

Cambridge University Press
The Edinburgh Building, Cambridge CB2 8RU, UK

Published in the United States of America by Cambridge University Press, New York

www.cambridge.org
Information on this title: www.cambridge.org/9781107698826

First published 1922
Re-issued 2013

A catalogue record for this publication is available from the British Library

ISBN 978-1-107-69882-6 Paperback

NOTE

RICHARD HOOKER (1553–1600) in his *The Laws of
Ecclesiastical Polity* left to the English race not only
a noble model of Christian controversy, but a great
exemplar of English Prose. The Preface which is here
given, addressed to "those who seek (as they term it)
the reformation of the Laws and Orders Ecclesiastical in
the Church of England" was published, with the first
four books, in 1594 when he had retired from the
Mastership of the Temple at his own request, "weary
of the noise and oppositions of this place; and, indeed,
GOD and Nature did not intend me for contentions, but
for study and quietness." The opportunity for study
and quietness he found first in his Rectory of Bos-
combe near Amesbury (1591–1595) and afterwards as
Rector of Bishopsbourne near Canterbury, where he
died in 1600.

The object of the Preface is to secure a hearing for
the great argument of the main treatise. The theory
and practice embodied in "The Laws and Orders
Ecclesiastical of the Church of England" were in
danger of going by default: the Puritan position had
been steadily gaining in prestige owing to the out-
standing reputation of Calvin and the presumption
widely occupying the minds of English Christians that
in that position was to be found the only strong bulwark
against the pretensions of the Church of Rome. In the
Preface, then, Hooker (c. ii) narrates the origin and
examines the causes of the reputation of Calvin as main
author of the Puritan Discipline: and (c. iii) explores
the ways by which the claim of that Discipline to be
the only Scriptural and right Order had been established in men's minds. He (cc. iv–vii) argues that these

ways were not such as to preclude the chance of error or to bar the necessity of further enquiry; and (c. viii) he finally enforces the necessity of such an enquiry by an examination of the consequences, which had been deduced from the arguments of the assertors of this Discipline and exhibited in the history of the Anabaptists.

This brief account may give the reader of the following pages a guide to the development of the argument and enable him the better to appreciate the qualities of Hooker's prose. " In wealth and stateliness and strength of diction Hooker stands indisputably in the first rank of English writers: but there are also humbler and more imitable characteristics to be studied in his ways of self-expression.... Hooker's language... may seem obscure if his reader is unable or unwilling to read slowly and to take pains; but the obscurity is the obscurity of depth and not of turbidness. No trouble has been grudged to find the words that may exactly tell the thought, in all its fulness and with all its necessary qualification; and in the present day, when not only he who reads must run, but he who writes is generally running too, there is a wholesome discipline and also an unusual satisfaction to be found in studying an author whose every sentence has been thoroughly and conscientiously thought out, who is never slovenly, or tautologous, and for whose work the most noble language seems somehow the most serviceable and appropriate[1]."

R. St J. P.

Whitsuntide, 1922.

[1] Bp Paget, Introduction to Book V of the Ecclesiastical Polity, p. 3.

A
PREFACE

To them that seek (as they term it)

THE REFORMATION OF THE LAWS

AND

ORDERS ECCLESIASTICAL

IN THE

CHURCH OF ENGLAND

THOUGH for no other cause, yet for this; that posterity
may know we have not loosely through silence per-
mitted things to pass away as in a dream, there shall
be for men's information extant thus much concerning
the present state of the Church of God established
amongst us, and their careful endeavour which would
have upheld the same. At your hands, beloved in our
Lord and Saviour Jesus Christ (for in him the love
which we bear unto all that would but seem to be
born of him, it is not the sea of your gall and bitterness
that shall ever drown,) I have no great cause to look
for other than the selfsame portion and lot, which
your manner hath been hitherto to lay on them that
concur not in opinion and sentence with you. But
our hope is, that the God of peace shall (notwithstanding man's nature too impatient of contumelious
malediction) enable us quietly and even gladly to
suffer all things, for that work sake which we covet to
perform.

The wonderful zeal and fervour wherewith ye have
withstood the received orders of this church, was the
first thing which caused me to enter into consideration, whether (as all your published books and writings

peremptorily maintain) every Christian man, fearing
God, stand bound to join with you for the furtherance
of that which ye term *the Lord's Discipline*. Wherein
I must plainly confess unto you, that before I examined
your sundry declarations in that behalf, it could not
settle in my head to think, but that undoubtedly such
numbers of otherwise right well affected and most
religiously inclined minds had some marvellous reasonable inducements, which led them with so great
earnestness that way. But when once, as near as my
slender ability would serve, I had with travail and
care performed that part of the Apostle's advice and
counsel in such cases, whereby he willeth to "try all
things," and was come at the length so far, that there
remained only the other clause to be satisfied, wherein
he concludeth that "what good is must be held;"
there was in my poor understanding no remedy, but
to set down this as my final resolute persuasion:
"Surely the present form of church-government
which the laws of this land have established is such,
as no law of God nor reason of man hath hitherto been
alleged of force sufficient to prove they do ill, who to
the uttermost of their power withstand the alteration
thereof." Contrariwise, "The other, which instead
of it we are required to accept, is only by error and
misconceit named the ordinance of Jesus Christ, no
one proof as yet brought forth whereby it may clearly
appear to be so in very deed."

The explication of which two things I have here
thought good to offer into your own hands, heartily
beseeching you even by the meekness of Jesus Christ,
whom I trust ye love; that, as ye tender the peace and
quietness of this church, if there be in you that gracious

humility which hath ever been the crown and glory of a Christianly-disposed mind, if your own souls, hearts, and consciences (the sound integrity whereof can but hardly stand with the refusal of truth in personal respects) be, as I doubt not but they are, things most dear and precious unto you: "Let not the faith which ye have in our Lord Jesus Christ" be blemished "with partialities[1];" regard not who it is which speaketh, but weigh only what is spoken. Think not that ye read the words of one who bendeth himself as an adversary against the truth which ye have already embraced; but the words of one who desireth even to embrace together with you the selfsame truth, if it be the truth; and for that cause (for no other, God he knoweth) hath undertaken the burdensome labour of this painful kind of conference. For the plainer access whereunto, let it be lawful for me to rip up to the very bottom, how and by whom your discipline was planted, at such time as this age we live in began to make first trial thereof.

II. A founder[2] it had, whom, for mine own part, I think incomparably the wisest man that ever the French church did enjoy, since the hour it enjoyed him. His bringing up was in the study of the civil law. Divine knowledge he gathered, not by hearing or reading so much, as by teaching others. For, though thousands were debtors to him, as touching knowledge in that kind; yet he to none but only to God, the author of that most blessed fountain, the Book of Life, and of the admirable dexterity of wit, together with the helps of other learning which were his guides: till being occasioned to leave France, he

[1] James ii. 1.   [2] Calvin.

fell at the length upon Geneva; which city the bishop
and clergy thereof had a little before (as some do
affirm) forsaken, being of likelihood frighted with the
people's sudden attempt for abolishment of Popish
religion: the event of which enterprize they thought
it not safe for themselves to wait for in that place. At
the coming of Calvin thither, the form of their civil
regiment was popular, as it continueth at this day:
neither king, nor duke, nor nobleman of any authority
or power over them, but officers chosen by the people
yearly out of themselves, to order all things with
public consent. For spiritual government, they had
no laws at all agreed upon, but did what the pastors
of their souls by persuasion could win them unto.
Calvin, being admitted one of their preachers, and
a divinity reader amongst them, considered how
dangerous it was that the whole estate of that church
should hang still on so slender a thread, as the liking
of an ignorant multitude is, if it have power to change
whatsoever itself listeth. Wherefore taking unto him
two of the other ministers for more countenance of
the action, (albeit the rest were all against it,) they
moved, and in the end persuaded with much ado, the
people to bind themselves by solemn oath, first never
to admit the Papacy amongst them again; and secondly,
to live in obedience unto such orders concerning the
exercise of their religion, and the form of their ecclesiastical government, as those their true and faithful
ministers of God's word had agreeably to scripture
set down for that end and purpose[1]

When these things began to be put in ure, the
people also (what causes moving them thereunto,
themselves best know) began to repent them of that

they had done, and irefully to champ upon the bit
they had taken into their mouths; the rather, for that
they grew by means of this innovation into dislike
with some churches near about them, the benefit of
whose good friendship their state could not well lack.
It was the manner of those times (whether through
men's desire to enjoy alone the glory of their own
enterprizes, or else because the quickness of their
occasions required present dispatch; so it was) that
every particular church did that within itself, which
some few of their own thought good, by whom the
rest were all directed. Such number of churches then
being, though free within themselves, yet small,
common conference beforehand might have eased
them of much after trouble. But a greater inconvenience it bred, that every later endeavoured to be certain
degrees more removed from conformity with the church
of Rome, than the rest before had been: whereupon
grew marvellous great dissimilitudes, and by reason
thereof, jealousies, heart-burnings, jars and discords
amongst them. Which, notwithstanding, might have
easily been prevented, if the orders, which each church
did think fit and convenient for itself, had not so
peremptorily been established under that high com-
manding form, which tendered them unto the people,
as things everlastingly required by the law of that
Lord of Lords, against whose statutes there is no
exception to be taken. For by this mean it came to
pass, that one church could not but accuse and condemn another of disobedience to the will of Christ,
in those things where manifest difference was between
them: whereas the selfsame orders allowed, but yet
established in more wary and suspense manner, as

being to stand in force till God should give the opportunity of some general conference what might be best for every of them afterwards to do; this I say had both prevented all occasion of just dislike which others might take, and reserved a greater liberty unto the authors themselves of entering into farther consultation afterwards. Which though never so necessary they could not easily now admit, without some fear of derogation from their credit: and therefore that which once they had done, they became for ever after resolute to maintain.

Calvin therefore and the other two his associates, stiffly refusing to administer the holy Communion to such as would not quietly, without contradiction and murmur, submit themselves unto the orders which their solemn oath had bound them to obey, were in that quarrel banished the town.

A few years after (such was the levity of that people) the places of one or two of their ministers being fallen void, they were not before so willing to be rid of their learned pastor, as now importunate to obtain him again from them who had given him entertainment, and which were loath to part with him, had not unresistable earnestness been used. One of the town ministers, that saw in what manner the people were bent for the revocation of Calvin, gave him notice of their affection in this sort[1]. "The senate of two hundred being assembled, they all crave Calvin. The next day a general convocation; they cry in like sort again all, We will have Calvin, that good and learned man, Christ's minister. This," saith he, "when I understood, I could not choose but praise God, nor was I able to judge otherwise than that 'this was the Lord's

[1] Epist. Cal. 24.

doing, and that it was marvellous in our eyes,' and that 'the stone which the builders refused, was now made the head of the corner[1].'" The other two whom they had thrown out, (together with Calvin,) they were content should enjoy their exile. Many causes might lead them to be more desirous of him. First, his yielding unto them in one thing might happily put them in hope, that time would breed the like easiness of condescending further unto them. For in his absence he had persuaded them, with whom he was able to prevail, that albeit himself did better like of common bread to be used in the Eucharist, yet the other they rather should accept, than cause any trouble in the Church about it. Again, they saw that the name of Calvin waxed every day greater abroad, and that together with his fame, their infamy was spread, which had so rashly and childishly ejected him. Besides, it was not unlikely but that his credit in the world might many ways stand the poor town in great stead: as the truth is, their minister's foreign estimation hitherto hath been the best stake in their hedge. But whatsoever secret respects were likely to move them; for contenting of their minds Calvin returned (as it had been another Tully) to his old home.

He ripely considered how gross a thing it were for men of his quality, wise and grave men, to live with such a multitude, and to be tenants at will under them, as their ministers, both himself and others, had been. For the remedy of which inconvenience, he gave them plainly to understand, that if he did become their teacher again, they must be content to admit a complete form of discipline, which both they and also

[1] Luke xx. 17.

their pastors should now be solemnly sworn to observe for ever after. Of which discipline the main and principal parts were these: A standing ecclesiastical court to be established; perpetual judges in that court to be their ministers; others of the people to be annually chosen (twice so many in number as they) to be judges together with them in the same court: these two sorts to have the care of all men's manners, power of determining all kind of ecclesiastical causes, and authority to convent, to control, to punish, as far as with excommunication, whomsoever they should think worthy, none either small or great excepted.

This device I see not how the wisest at that time living could have bettered, if we duly consider what the present estate of Geneva did then require. For their bishop and his clergy being (as it is said) departed from them by moonlight, or howsoever, being departed; to choose in his room any other bishop, had been a thing altogether impossible. And for their ministers to seek that themselves alone might have coercive power over the whole church, would perhaps have been hardly construed at that time. But when so frank an offer was made, that for every one minister there should be two of the people to sit and give voice in the ecclesiastical consistory, what inconvenience could they easily find which themselves might not be liable always to remedy?

Howbeit (as evermore the simpler sort are, even when they see no apparent cause, jealous notwithstanding over the secret intents and purposes of wiser men) this proposition of his did somewhat trouble them. Of the ministers themselves which had stayed behind in the city when Calvin was gone, some, upon

knowledge of the people's earnest intent to recall him
to his place again, had beforehand written their letters
of submission, and assured him of their allegiance
for ever after, if it should like him to hearken unto
that public suit. But yet misdoubting what might
happen, if this discipline did go forward; they objected
against it the example of other reformed churches
living quietly and orderly without it. Some of chiefest
place and countenance amongst the laity professed
with greater stomach their judgments, that such a
discipline was little better than Popish tyranny dis-
guised and tendered unto them under a new form.
This sort, it may be, had some fear, that the filling
up of the seats in the consistory with so great a number
of laymen was but to please the minds of the people,
to the end they might think their own sway somewhat;
but when things came to trial of practice, their pastors'
learning would be at all times of force to over-persuade
simple men, who knowing the time of their own presi-
dentship to be but short would always stand in fear
of their ministers' perpetual authority: and among the
ministers themselves, one being so far in estimation
above the rest, the voices of the rest were likely to be
given for the most part respectively, with a kind of
secret dependency and awe: so that in show a marvellous indifferently composed senate ecclesiastical
was to govern, but in effect one only man should, as
the spirit and soul of the residue, do all in all. But
what did these vain surmises boot? Brought they
were now to so strait an issue, that of two things
they must choose one: namely, whether they would
to their endless disgrace, with ridiculous lightness
dismiss him whose restitution they had in so impotent

manner desired; or else condescend unto that demand, wherein he was resolute either to have it, or to leave them. They thought it better to be somewhat hardly yoked at home, than for ever abroad discredited. Wherefore in the end those orders were on all sides assented unto: with no less alacrity of mind than cities unable to hold out longer are wont to shew, when they take conditions such as it liketh him to offer them which hath them in the narrow straits of advantage.

Not many years were over-passed, before these twice-sworn men adventured to give their last and hottest assault to the fortress of the same discipline; childishly granting by common consent of their whole senate, and that under their town seal, a relaxation to one Bertelier, whom the eldership had excommunicated: further also decreeing, with strange absurdity, that to the same senate it should belong to give final judgment in matter of excommunication, and to absolve whom it pleased them: clean contrary to their own former deeds and oaths. The report of which decree being forthwith brought unto Calvin; "Before," saith he, "this decree take place, either my blood or banishment shall sign it." Again, two days before the communion should be celebrated, his speech was publickly to like effect: "Kill me if ever this hand do reach forth the things that are holy to them whom The Church hath judged despisers." Whereupon, for fear of tumult, the forenamed Bertelier was by his friends advised for that time not to use the liberty granted him by the senate, nor to present himself in the church, till they saw somewhat further what would ensue. After the communion quietly ministered, and some likelihood of peaceable ending of these troubles

without any more ado, that very day in the afternoon,
besides all men's expectation, concluding his ordinary
sermon, he telleth them, that because he neither had
learned nor taught to strive with such as are in
authority, "therefore," saith he, "the case so standing
as now it doth, let me use these words of the apostle
unto you, 'I commend you unto God and the word
of his grace;'" and so bade them heartily all adieu.

It sometimes cometh to pass, that the readiest way
which a wise man hath to conquer, is to fly. This
voluntary and unexpected mention of sudden departure caused presently the senate (for according to
their wonted manner they still continued only constant
in unconstancy) to gather themselves together, and
for a time to suspend their own decree, leaving things
to proceed as before till they had heard the judgment
of four Helvetian cities concerning the matter which
was in strife. This to have done at the first before they
gave assent unto any order had shewed some wit and
discretion in them: but now to do it was as much as to
say in effect, that they would play their parts on a
stage. Calvin therefore dispatcheth with all expedi-
tion his letters unto some principal pastor in every of
those cities, craving earnestly at their hands, to respect
this cause as a thing whereupon the whole state of
religion and piety in that church did so much depend,
that God and all good men were now inevitably certain
to be trampled under foot, unless those four cities
by their good means might be brought to give sentence with the ministers of Geneva, when the cause
should be brought before them: yea so to give it,
that two things it might effectually contain; the one
an absolute approbation of the discipline of Geneva

as consonant unto the word of God, without any cautions, qualifications, if's or and's; the other an earnest admonition not to innovate or change the same. His vehement request herein as touching both points was satisfied. For albeit the said Helvetian churches did never as yet observe that discipline, nevertheless, the senate of Geneva having required their judgment concerning these three questions: First, "After what manner, by God's commandment, according to the scripture and unspotted religion, excommunication is to be exercised:" Secondly, "Whether it may not be exercised some other way than by the consistory:" Thirdly, "What the use of their churches was to do in this case[1]:" answer was returned from the said churches, "That they had heard already of those consistorial laws, and did acknowledge them to be *godly* ordinances *drawing towards* the prescript of the work of God; for which cause they did not think it good for *the Church of Geneva* by innovation to change the same, but rather to keep them as they were." Which answer, although not answering unto the former demands, but respecting what Master Calvin had judged requisite for them to answer, was notwithstanding accepted without any further reply: in as much as they plainly saw, that when stomach doth strive with wit, the match is not equal. And so the heat of their former contentions began to slake.

The present inhabitants of Geneva, I hope, will not take it in evil part, that the faultiness of their people heretofore is by us so far forth laid open, as their own learned guides and pastors have thought

[1] Epist. 166.

necessary to discover it unto the world. For out of their books and writings it is that I have collected this whole narration, to the end it might thereby appear in what sort amongst them that discipline was planted, for which so much contention is raised amongst ourselves. The reason which moved Calvin herein to be so earnest, was, as Beza himself testifieth[1], "For that he saw how needful these bridles were, to be put in the jaws of that city." That which by wisdom he saw to be requisite for that people, was by as great wisdom compassed.

But wise men are men, and the truth is truth. That which Calvin did for establishment of his discipline, seemeth more commendable than that which he taught for the countenancing of it established. Nature worketh in us all a love to our own counsels. The contradiction of others is a fan to inflame that love. Our love set on fire to maintain that which once we have done, sharpeneth the wit to dispute, to argue, and by all means to reason for it. Wherefore a marvel it were if a man of so great capacity, having such incitements to make him desirous of all kind of furtherances unto his cause, could espy in the whole Scripture of God nothing which might breed at the least a probable opinion of likelihood, that divine authority itself was the same way somewhat inclinable. And all which the wit even of Calvin was able from thence to draw, by sifting the very utmost sentence and syllable, is no more than that certain speeches there are which to him did seem to intimate that all Christian churches ought to have their elderships endued with power of excommunication, and that a part of those elderships

[1] "Quod eam urbem videret omnino his frænis indigere."

every where should be chosen out from amongst the laity, after that form which himself had framed Geneva unto. But what argument are ye able to shew, whereby it was ever proved by Calvin, that any one sentence of Scripture doth necessarily enforce these things, or the rest wherein your opinion concurreth with his against the orders of your own church?

We should be injurious unto virtue itself, if we did derogate from them whom their industry hath made great. Two things of principal moment there are which have deservedly procured him honour throughout the world: the one his exceeding pains in composing the Institutions of Christian religion; the other his no less industrious travails for exposition of holy Scripture according unto the same Institutions. In which two things whosoever they were that after him bestowed their labour, he gained the advantage of prejudice against them, if they gainsayed; and of glory above them, if they consented. His writings published after the question about that discipline was once begun omit not any the least occasion of extolling the use and singular necessity thereof. Of what account the Master of Sentences[1] was in the church of Rome, the same and more amongst the preachers of reformed churches Calvin had purchased; so that the perfectest divines were judged they, which were skilfullest in Calvin's writings. His books almost the very canon to judge both doctrine and discipline by. French churches, both under others abroad and at home in their own country, all cast according to that mould which Calvin had made. The church of Scotland in erecting the fabric of their reformation took the self-

[1] Peter Lombard.

same pattern. Till at length the discipline, which was at the first so weak, that without the staff of their approbation, who were not subject unto it themselves, it had not brought others under subjection, began now to challenge universal obedience, and to enter into open conflict with those very churches, which in desperate extremity had been relievers of it.

To one of those churches which lived in most peaceable sort, and abounded as well with men for their learning in other professions singular, as also with divines whose equals were not elsewhere to be found, a church ordered by Gualter's discipline, and not by that which Geneva adoreth; unto this church, the Church of Heidelburgh, there cometh one who craving leave to dispute publicly defendeth with open disdain of their government, that "to a minister with his eldership power is given by the law of God to excommunicate whomsoever, yea even kings and princes themselves." Here were the seeds sown of that controversy which sprang up between Beza and Erastus about the matter of excommunication, whether there ought to be in all churches an eldership having power to excommunicate, and a part of that eldership to be of necessity certain chosen out from amongst the laity for that purpose. In which disputation they have, as to me it seemeth, divided very equally the truth between them; Beza most truly maintaining the necessity of excommunication, Erastus as truly the non-necessity of lay-elders to be ministers thereof.

Amongst ourselves, there was in King Edward's days some question moved by reason of a few men's scrupulosity touching certain things. And beyond seas, of them which fled in the days of Queen Mary,

some contenting themselves abroad with the use of
their own service-book at home authorized before their
departure out of the realm, others liking better the
Common Prayer-book of the Church of Geneva trans-
lated, those smaller contentions before begun were by
this means somewhat increased. Under the happy
reign of her Majesty which now is, the greatest matter
awhile contended for was the wearing of the cap and
surplice, till there came Admonitions directed unto
the high court of Parliament, by men who concealing
their names thought it glory enough to discover their
minds and affections, which now were universally bent
even against all the orders and laws, wherein this
church is found unconformable to the platform of
Geneva. Concerning the Defender[1] of which Admonitions, all that I mean to say is but this: *there will
come a time when three words uttered with charity
and meekness shall receive a far more blessed reward
than three thousand volumes written with disdainful
sharpness of wit*. But the manner of men's writing
must not alienate our hearts from the truth, if it
appear they have the truth; as the followers of the
same defender do think he hath; and in that persuasion
they follow him, no otherwise than himself doth
Calvin, Beza, and others, with the like persuasion
that they in this cause had the truth. We being as
fully persuaded otherwise, it resteth that some kind
of trial be used to find out which part is in error.

III. The first mean whereby nature teacheth men
to judge good from evil, as well in laws as in other
things, is the force of their own discretion. Hereunto
therefore St. Paul referreth oftentimes his own speech,

[1] Thomas Cartwright.

to be considered of by them that heard him. "I speak as to them which have understanding, judge ye what I say[1]." Again afterward, "Judge in yourselves, is it comely that a woman pray uncovered[2]?" The exercise of this kind of judgment our Saviour requireth in the Jews[3]. In them of Berea the Scripture commendeth it[4]. Finally, whatsoever we do, if our own secret judgment consent not unto it as fit and good to be done, the doing of it to us is sin, although the thing itself be allowable. St. Paul's rule therefore generally is, "Let every man in his own mind be fully persuaded of that thing which he either alloweth or doth[5]."

Some things are so familiar and plain, that truth from falsehood, and good from evil, is most easily discerned in them, even by men of no deep capacity. And of that nature, for the most part, are things absolutely unto all men's salvation necessary, either to be held or denied, either to be done or avoided. For which cause St. Augustine acknowledgeth, that they are not only set down, but also plainly set down in Scripture; so that he which heareth or readeth may without any great difficulty understand. Other things also there are belonging (though in a lower degree of importance) unto the offices of Christian men: which, because they are more obscure, more intricate and hard to be judged of, therefore God hath appointed some to spend their whole time principally in the study of things divine, to the end that in these more doubtful cases their understanding might be a light to direct others. "If the understanding power or

[1] 1 Cor. x. 15.   [2] *Ibid*. xi. 13.
[3] Luke xii. 56, 57.   [4] Acts xvii. 11.
[5] Rom. xiv. 5.

faculty of the soul be" (saith the grand physician[1])
"like unto bodily sight, not of equal sharpness in all,
what can be more convenient than that, even as the
dark-sighted man is directed by the clear about things
visible; so likewise in matters of deeper discourse the
wise in heart do shew the simple where his way lieth?"
In our doubtful cases of law, what man is there who
seeth not how requisite it is that professors of skill in
that faculty be our directors? So it is in all other kinds
of knowledge. And even in this kind likewise the Lord
hath himself appointed, that "the priest's lips should
preserve knowledge, and that other men should seek
the truth at his mouth, *because* he is the messenger
of the Lord of hosts[2]." Gregory Nazianzen, offended
at the people's too great presumption in controlling
the judgment of them to whom in such cases they
should have rather submitted their own, seeketh by
earnest entreaty to stay them within their bounds:
"Presume not ye that are sheep to make yourselves
guides of them that should guide you; neither seek
ye to overskip the fold which they about you have
pitched. It sufficeth for your part, if ye can well frame
yourselves to be ordered. Take not upon you to judge
your judges, nor to make them subject to your laws
who should be a law to you; for God is not a God of
sedition and confusion, but of order and of peace[3]."
But ye will say that if the guides of the people be
blind, the common sort of men must not close up their
own eyes and be led by the conduct of such[4]: if the
priest be "partial in the law[5]," the flock must not

---

[1] Galen. de opt. docen. gen.　　　[2] Mal. ii. 7.
[3] Greg. Nazian. Orat. qua se excusat.
[4] Matt. xv. 14.　　　　　　　　　[5] Mal. ii. 9.

therefore depart from the ways of sincere truth, and in
simplicity yield to be followers of him for his place
sake and office over them. Which thing, though in
itself most true, is in your defence notwithstanding
weak; because the matter wherein ye think that ye
see, and imagine that your ways are sincere, is of far
deeper consideration than any one amongst five hundred of you conceiveth. Let the vulgar sort amongst
you know, that there is not the least branch of the
cause wherein they are so resolute, but to the trial of
it a great deal more appertaineth than their conceit
doth reach unto. I write not this in disgrace of the
simplest that way given, but I would gladly they knew
the nature of that cause wherein they think themselves
thoroughly instructed and are not; by means whereof
they daily run themselves, without feeling their own
hazard, upon the dint of the apostles' sentence against
"evil-speakers as touching things wherein they are
ignorant[1]."

If it be granted a thing unlawful for private men,
not called unto public consultation, to dispute which
is the best state of civil polity[2], (with a desire of bringing
in some other kind, than that under which they already
live, for of such disputes I take it his meaning was;)
if it be a thing confessed, that of such questions they
cannot determine without rashness, inasmuch as a
great part of them consisteth in special circumstances,
and for one kind as many reasons may be brought as
for another; is there any reason in the world, why
they should better judge what kind of regiment
ecclesiastical is the fittest? For in the civil state more

[1] Jude 10; 2 Pet. ii. 12.
[2] Calvin, Instit. lib. iv. cap. xx. § 8.

insight, and in those affairs more experience a great deal must needs be granted them, than in this they can possibly have. When they which write in defence of your discipline and commend it unto the Highest not in the least cunning manner, are forced notwithstanding to acknowledge, "that with whom the truth is they know not[1]," they are not certain; what certainty or knowledge can the multitude have thereof?

Weigh what doth move the common sort so much to favour this innovation, and it shall soon appear unto you, that the force of particular reasons which for your several opinions are alleged is a thing whereof the multitude never did nor could so consider as to be therewith wholly carried; but certain general inducements are used to make saleable your cause in gross; and when once men have cast a fancy towards it, any slight declaration of specialties will serve to lead forward men's inclinable and prepared minds.

The method of winning the people's affection unto a general liking of "the cause" (for so ye term it) hath been this. First, In the hearing of the multitude, the faults especially of higher callings are ripped up with marvellous exceeding severity and sharpness of reproof; which being oftentimes done begetteth a great good opinion of integrity, zeal, and holiness, to such constant reprovers of sin, as by likelihood would never be so much offended at that which is evil, unless themselves were singularly good.

The next thing hereunto is, to impute all faults and corruptions, wherewith the world aboundeth, unto the kind of ecclesiastical government established.

[1] The Author of the Petition directed to her Majesty, p. 3.

Wherein, as before by reproving faults they purchased unto themselves with the multitude a name to be virtuous; so by finding out this kind of cause they obtain to be judged wise above others: whereas in truth unto the form even of Jewish government, which the Lord himself (they all confess) did establish, with like show of reason they might impute those faults which the prophets condemn in the governors of that commonwealth, as to the English kind of regiment ecclesiastical, (whereof also God himself though in another sort is author,) the stains and blemishes found in our state; which springing from the root of human frailty and corruption, not only are, but have been always more or less, yea and (for any thing we know to the contrary) will be till the world's end complained of, what form of government soever take place.

Having gotten thus much sway in the hearts of men, a third step is to propose their own form of church-government, as the only sovereign remedy of all evils; and to adorn it with all the glorious titles that may be. And the nature, as of men that have sick bodies, so likewise of the people in the crazedness of their minds possessed with dislike and discontentment at things present, is to imagine that any thing, the virtue whereof they hear commended, would help them; but that most, which they least have tried.

The fourth degree of inducement is by fashioning the very notions and conceits of men's minds in such sort, that when they read the Scripture, they may think that every thing soundeth towards the advancement of that discipline, and to the utter disgrace of the contrary. Pythagoras, by bringing up his scholars in the speculative knowledge of numbers, made their

conceits therein so strong, that when they came to
the contemplation of things natural, they imagined
that in every particular thing they even beheld as it
were with their eyes, how the elements of number gave
essence and being to the works of nature: a thing in
reason impossible; which notwithstanding, through
their misfashioned preconceit, appeared unto them
no less certain, than if nature had written it in the
very foreheads of all the creatures of God[1]. When
they of the "Family of Love" have it once in their
heads, that Christ doth not signify any one person,
but a quality whereof many are partakers; that to be
"raised" is nothing else but to be regenerated, or
endued with the said quality; and that when separation of them which have it from them which have it
not is here made, this is "judgment:" how plainly
do they imagine that the Scripture every where
speaketh in the favour of that sect? And assuredly,
the very cause which maketh the simple and ignorant
to think they even see how the word of God runneth
currently on your side, is, that their minds are fore-
stalled and their conceits perverted beforehand, by
being taught, that an "elder" doth signify a layman
admitted only to the office or rule of government in
the Church; a "doctor," one which may only teach,
and neither preach nor administer the Sacraments;
a "deacon," one which hath charge of the alms-box,
and of nothing else: that the "sceptre," the "rod,"
the "throne" and "kingdom" of Christ, are a form
of regiment, only by pastors, elders, doctors, and
deacons; that by mystical resemblance Mount Sion
and Jerusalem are the churches which admit, Samaria

[1] Arist. Metaph. lib. i. cap. 5.

and Babylon the churches which oppugn the same form of regiment. And in like sort they are taught to apply all things spoken of repairing the walls and decayed parts of the city and temple of God, by Esdras, Nehemias, and the rest; as if purposely the Holy Ghost had therein meant to foresignify, what the authors of Admonitions to the Parliament, of Supplications to the Council, of Petitions to her Majesty, and of such other-like writs, should either do or suffer in behalf of this their cause.

From hence they proceed to a higher point, which is the persuading of men credulous and over-capable of such pleasing errors, that it is the special illumination of the Holy Ghost, whereby they discern those things in the word, which others reading yet discern them not. "Dearly beloved," saith St. John, "give not credit unto every spirit[1]." There are but two ways whereby the Spirit leadeth men into all truth; the one extraordinary, the other common; the one belonging but unto some few, the other extending itself unto all that are of God; the one, that which we call by a special divine excellency Revelation, the other Reason. If the Spirit by such revelation have discovered unto them the secrets of that discipline out of Scripture, they must profess themselves to be all (even men, women, and children) Prophets. Or if reason be the hand which the Spirit hath led them by; forasmuch as persuasions grounded upon reason are either weaker or stronger according to the force of those reasons whereupon the same are grounded, they must every of them from the greatest to the least be able for every several article to shew some special reason as

[1] 1 John iv. 1.

strong as their persuasion therein is earnest. Otherwise how can it be but that some other sinews there are from which that overplus of strength in persuasion doth arise? Most sure it is, that when men's affections do frame their opinions, they are in defence of error more earnest a great deal, than (for the most part) sound believers in the maintenance of truth apprehended according to the nature of that evidence which scripture yieldeth: which being in some things plain, as in the principles of Christian doctrine; in some things, as in these matters of discipline, more dark and doubtful; frameth correspondently that inward assent which God's most gracious Spirit worketh by it as by his effectual instrument. It is not therefore the fervent earnestness of their persuasion, but the soundness of those reasons whereupon the same is built, which must declare their opinions in these things to have been wrought by the Holy Ghost, and not by the fraud of that evil spirit, which is even in his illusions strong[1].

After that the fancy of the common sort hath once thoroughly apprehended the Spirit to be author of their persuasions concerning discipline; then is instilled into their hearts, that the same Spirit leading men into this opinion doth thereby seal them to be God's children; and that, as the state of the times now standeth, the most special token to know them that are God's own from others is an earnest affection that way. This hath bred high terms of separation between such and the rest of the world; whereby the one sort are named The brethren, The godly, and so forth; the other, worldlings, time-servers, pleasers of men not of God, with such like.

[1] 2 Thess. ii. 11.

From hence, they are easily drawn on to think it exceeding necessary, for fear of quenching that good Spirit, to use all means whereby the same may be both strengthened in themselves, and made manifest unto others. This maketh them diligent hearers of such as are known that way to incline; this maketh them eager to take and to seek all occasions of secret conference with such; this maketh them glad to use such as counsellors and directors in all their dealings which are of weight, as contracts, testaments, and the like; this maketh them, through an unweariable desire of receiving instruction from the masters of that company, to cast off the care of those very affairs which do most concern their estate, and to think that then they are like unto Mary, commendable for making choice of the better part. Finally, this is it which maketh them willing to charge, yea, oftentimes even to overcharge themselves, for such men's sustenance and relief, lest their zeal to the cause should any way be unwitnessed. For what is it which poor beguiled souls will not do through so powerful incitements?

In which respect it is also noted, that most labour hath been bestowed to win and retain towards this cause them whose judgments are commonly weakest by reason of their sex. And although not "women loden with sins[1]," as the apostle Saint Paul speaketh, but (as we verily esteem of them for the most part) women propense and inclinable to holiness be otherwise edified in good things, rather than carried away as captives into any kind of sin and evil, by such as enter into their houses with purpose to plant there a zeal and a love towards this kind of discipline: yet

[1] 2 Tim. iii. 6.

some occasion is hereby ministered for men to think, that if the cause which is thus furthered did gain by the soundness of proof whereupon it doth build itself, it would not most busily endeavour to prevail where least ability of judgment is: and therefore, that this so eminent industry in making proselytes more of that sex than of the other groweth, for that they are deemed apter to serve as instruments and helps in the cause. Apter they are through the eagerness of their affection, that maketh them, which way soever they take, diligent in drawing their husbands, children, servants, friends and allies the same way; apter through that natural inclination unto pity, which breedeth in them a greater readiness than in men to be bountiful towards their preachers who suffer want; apter through sundry opportunities, which they especially have, to procure encouragements for their brethren; finally, apter through a singular delight which they take in giving very large and particular intelligence, how all near about them stand affected as concerning the same cause.

But be they women or be they men, if once they have tasted of that cup, let any man of contrary opinion open his mouth to persuade them, they close up their ears, his reasons they weigh not, all is answered with rehearsal of the words of John, "'We are of God; he that knoweth God heareth us[1]:' as for the rest, ye are of the world; for this world's pomp and vanity it is that ye speak, and the world, whose ye are, heareth you." Which cloak sitteth no less fit on the back of their cause, than of the Anabaptists, when the dignity, authority and honour of

[1] 1 John iv. 6.

God's magistrate is upheld against them. Shew these
eagerly-affected men their inability to judge of such
matters; their answer is, "God hath chosen the
simple[1]." Convince them of folly, and that so plainly,
that very children upbraid them with it; they have
their bucklers of like defence: "Christ's own apostle
was accounted mad: the best men evermore by the
sentence of the world have been judged to be out of
their right minds[2]."

When instruction doth them no good, let them
feel but the least degree of most mercifully-tempered
severity, they fasten on the head of the Lord's vice-
gerents here on earth whatsoever they any where find
uttered against the cruelty of blood-thirsty men, and
to themselves they draw all the sentences which
scripture hath in the favour of innocency persecuted
for the truth; yea, they are of their due and deserved
sufferings no less proud, than those ancient disturbers
to whom Saint Augustine writeth, saying[3]: "Martyrs
rightly so named are they not which suffer for their
disorder, and for the ungodly breach they have made
of Christian unity, but which for righteousness' sake
are persecuted. For Agar also suffered persecution
at the hands of Sarah, wherein, she which did impose
was holy, and she unrighteous which did bear the
burden. In like sort, with thieves was the Lord himself crucified; but they, who were matched in the
pain which they suffered, were in the cause of their
sufferings disjoined."..."If that must needs be the

---

[1] 1 Cor. i. 27.
[2] Acts xxvi. 24. Sap. v. 14. "We fools thought his life
madness." (Merc. Tris. ad Æsculap.)
[3] Aug. Ep. 50.

true church which doth endure persecution, and not that which persecuteth, let them ask of the apostle what church Sarah did represent, when she held her maid in affliction. For even our mother which is free, the heavenly Jerusalem, that is to say, the true Church of God, was, as he doth affirm, prefigured in that very woman by whom the handmaid was so sharply handled. Although, if all things be thoroughly scanned, she did in truth more persecute Sarah by proud resistance, than Sarah her by severity of punishment."

These are the paths wherein ye have walked that are of the ordinary sort of men; these are the very steps ye have trodden, and the manifest degrees whereby ye are of your guides and directors trained up in that school: a custom of inuring your ears with reproof of faults especially in your governors; an use to attribute those faults to the kind of spiritual regiment under which ye live; boldness in warranting the force of their discipline for the cure of all such evils; a slight of framing your conceits to imagine that Scripture every where favoureth that discipline; persuasion that the cause why ye find it in Scripture is the illumination of the Spirit, that the same Spirit is a seal unto you of your nearness unto God, that ye are by all means to nourish and witness it in yourselves, and to strengthen on every side your minds against whatsoever might be of force to withdraw you from it.

IV. Wherefore to come unto you whose judgment is a lantern of direction for all the rest, you that frame thus the people's hearts, not altogether (as I willingly persuade myself) of a politic intent or purpose, but yourselves being first overborne with the weight of greater men's judgments: on your shoulders is laid the burden of upholding the cause by argument. For which purpose sentences out of the word of God ye allege divers: but so, that when the same are discussed, thus it always in a manner falleth out, that what things by virtue thereof ye urge upon us as altogether necessary, are found to be thence collected only by poor and marvellous slight conjectures. I need not give instance in any one sentence so alleged, for that I think the instance in any alleged otherwise a thing not easy to be given. A very strange thing sure it were, that such a discipline as ye speak of should be taught by Christ and his apostles in the word of God, and no church ever have found it out, nor received it till this present time; contrariwise, the government against which ye bend yourselves be observed every where throughout all generations and ages of the Christian world, no church ever perceiving the word of God to be against it. We require you to find out but one church upon the face of the whole earth, that hath been ordered by your discipline, or hath not been ordered by ours, that is to say, by episcopal regiment, sithence the time that the blessed Apostles were here conversant.

Many things out of antiquity ye bring, as if the purest times of the Church had observed the selfsame orders which you require; and as though your desire were that the churches of old should be patterns for us to follow, and even glasses, wherein we might see the practice of that which by you is gathered out of Scripture. But the truth is, ye mean nothing less. All this is done for fashion's sake only: for ye complain of it as of an injury, that men should be willed to seek

for examples and patterns of government in any of
those times that have been before[1]. Ye plainly hold,
that from the very Apostles' time till this present age,
wherein yourselves imagine ye have found out a right
pattern of sound discipline, there never was any time
safe to be followed. Which thing ye thus endeavour
to prove. "Out of Egesippus" ye say that "Eusebius[2]
writeth," how although "as long as the Apostles lived
the Church did remain a pure virgin, yet after the
death of the Apostles, and after they were once gone
whom God vouchsafed to make hearers of the divine
wisdom with their own ears, the placing of wicked
error began to come into the Church. Clement also
in a certain place, to confirm that there was corruption
of doctrine immediately after the Apostles' time,
allegeth the proverb, 'That there are few sons like
their fathers[3].' Socrates saith of the churches of
Rome and Alexandria[4], the most famous churches in
the Apostles' times, that about the year 430, the Roman
and Alexandrian bishops, leaving the sacred function,
were degenerate to a secular rule or dominion."
Hereupon ye conclude, that it is not safe to fetch our
government from any other than the Apostles' times.

Wherein by the way it may be noted, that in proposing the Apostles' times as a pattern for the Church
to follow, though the desire of you all be one, the
drift and purpose of you all is not one. The chiefest
thing which lay-reformers yawn for is, that the clergy
may through conformity in state and condition be
apostolical, poor as the Apostles of Christ were poor.

---

[1] T. C. lib. i. p. 97.   [2] Euseb. Hist. Eccles. lib. iii. cap. 32.
[3] Lib. Strom. somewhat after the beginning.
[4] Hist. Eccles. lib. vii. cap. 11.

In which one circumstance if they imagine so great perfection, they must think that church which hath such store of mendicant friars, a church in that respect most happy. Were it for the glory of God and the good of his Church indeed that the clergy should be left even as bare as the Apostles when they had neither staff nor script; that God, which should lay upon them the condition of his Apostles, would I hope endue them with the selfsame affection which was in that holy Apostle, whose words concerning his own right virtuous contentment of heart, "as well how to want, as how to abound[1]," are a most fit episcopal emprese. The Church of Christ is a body mystical. A body cannot stand, unless the parts thereof be proportionable. Let it therefore be required on both parts, at the hands of the clergy, to be in meanness of state like the Apostles; at the hand of the laity, to be as they were who lived under the Apostles: and in this reformation there will be, though little wisdom, yet some indifferency.

But your reformation which are of the clergy (if yet it displease you not that I should say ye are of the clergy) seemeth to aim at a broader mark. Ye think that he which will perfectly reform must bring the form of church-discipline unto the state which then it was at. A thing neither possible, nor certain, nor absolutely convenient.

Concerning the first, what was used in the Apostles' times, the Scripture fully declareth not; so that making their times the rule and canon of church-polity, ye make a rule, which being not possible to be fully known, is as impossible to be kept.

[1] Phil. iv. 12.

Again, sith the later even of the Apostles' own times had that which in the former was not thought upon; in this general proposing of the apostolical times, there is no certainty which should be followed: especially seeing that ye give us great cause to doubt how far ye allow those times. For albeit "the loover of antichristian building were not," ye say, as then "set up, yet the foundations thereof were secretly and under the ground laid in the Apostles' times:" so that all other times ye plainly reject, and the Apostles' own times ye approve with marvellous great suspicion, leaving it intricate and doubtful, wherein we are to keep ourselves unto the pattern of their times.

Thirdly, whereas it is the error of the common multitude to consider only what hath been of old, and if the same were well, to see whether still it continue; if not, to condemn that presently which is, and never to search upon what ground or consideration the change might grow: such rudeness cannot be in you so well borne with, whom learning and judgment hath enabled much more soundly to discern how far the times of the Church and the orders thereof may alter without offence. True it is, the ancienter[1], the better ceremonies of religion are; howbeit, not absolutely true and without exception; but true only so far forth as those different ages do agree in the state of those things, for which at the first those rites, orders, and ceremonies, were instituted. In the Apostles'

---

[1] "Antiquitas ceremoniis atque fanis tantum sanctitatis tribuere consuevit, quantum adstruxerit vetustatis." Arno. p. 746. [The words are from Minutius Felix, p. 4, line 30, ed. Elmenhorst. In many former editions, and no doubt in that which Hooker used, the dialogue of Minutius is ascribed to Arnobius.]

times that was harmless, which being now revived would be scandalous; as their *oscula sancta*[1]. Those feasts of charity[2], which being instituted by the Apostles, were retained in the Church long after, are not now thought any where needful. What man is there of understanding, unto whom it is not manifest how the way of providing for the clergy by tithes, the device of alms-houses for the poor, the sorting out of the people into their several parishes, together with sundry other things which the Apostles' times could not have, (being now established,) are much more convenient and fit for the Church of Christ, than if the same should be taken away for conformity's sake with the ancientest and first times?

The orders therefore, which were observed in the Apostles' times, are not to be urged as a rule universally either sufficient or necessary. If they be, nevertheless on your part it still remaineth to be better proved, that the form of discipline, which ye entitle apostolical, was in the Apostles' times exercised. For

[1] Rom. xvi. 16; 2 Cor. xiii. 12; 1 Thess. v. 26; 1 Pet. v. 14. In their meetings to serve God, their manner was, in the end to salute one another with a kiss; using these words, "Peace be with you." For which cause Tertullian doth call it, *signaculum orationis*, "the seal of prayer." Lib. de Orat.

[2] Epist. Jud. xii. Concerning which feasts, Saint Chrysostom saith, "Statis diebus mensas faciebant communes, et peracta synaxi post sacramentorum communionem inibant convivium, divitibus quidem cibos afferentibus, pauperibus autem et qui nihil habebant etiam vocatis." In 1 Cor. xi. 17, Hom. xxvii.

Of the same feasts, in like sort, Tertullian. "Cœna nostra de nomine rationem sui ostendit. Vocatur enim ἀγάπη, id quod est penes Græcos *dilectio*. Quantiscunque sumptibus constet, lucrum est pietatis nomine facere sumptum." Apol. cap. 39.

of this very thing ye fail even touching that which ye make most account of, as being matter of substance in discipline, I mean the power of your lay-elders, and the difference of your doctors from the pastors in all churches. So that in sum, we may be bold to conclude, that besides these last times, which for insolency, pride, and egregious contempt of all good order, are the worst, there are none wherein ye can truly affirm, that the complete form of your discipline, or the substance thereof, was practised.

The evidence therefore of antiquity failing you, ye fly to the judgments of such learned men, as seem by their writings to be of opinion, that all Christian churches should receive your discipline, and abandon ours. Wherein, as ye heap up the names of a number of men not unworthy to be had in honour; so there are a number whom when ye mention, although it serve you to purpose with the ignorant and vulgar sort, who measure by tale and not by weight, yet surely they who know what quality and value the men are of, will think ye draw very near the dregs. But were they all of as great account as the best and chiefest amongst them, with us notwithstanding neither are they, neither ought they to be of such reckoning, that their opinion or conjecture should cause the laws of the Church of England to give place. Much less when they neither do all agree in that opinion, and of them which are at agreement, the most part through a courteous inducement have followed one man as their guide, finally that one therein not unlikely to have swerved. If any one chance to say it is probable that in the Apostles' times there were lay-elders, or not to mislike the continuance of them in the Church, or to affirm that Bishops at the first were a name but not a power distinct from Presbyters, or to speak any thing in praise of those churches which are without episcopal regiment, or to reprove the fault of such as abuse that calling; all these ye register for men persuaded as you are, that every Christian church standeth bound by the law of God to put down bishops, and in their rooms to elect an eldership so authorized as you would have it for the government of each parish. Deceived greatly they are therefore, who think that all they whose names are cited amongst the favourers of this cause, are on any such verdict agreed.

Yet touching some material points of your discipline, a kind of agreement we grant there is amongst many divines of reformed churches abroad. For, first, to do as the Church of Geneva did the learned in some other churches must needs be the more willing, who having used in like manner not the slow and tedious help of proceeding by public authority, but the people's more quick endeavour for alteration, in such an exigent I see not well how they could have stayed to deliberate about any other regiment than that which already was devised to their hands, that which in like case had been taken, that which was easiest to be established without delay, that which was likeliest to content the people by reason of some kind of sway which it giveth them. When therefore the example of one church was thus at the first almost through a kind of constraint or necessity followed by many, their concurrence in persuasion about some material points belonging to the same polity is not strange. For we are not to marvel greatly, if they which have all done the same thing, do easily embrace the same opinion as concerning their own doings.

Besides, mark I beseech you that which Galen in matter of philosophy noteth[1]; for the like falleth out even in questions of higher knowledge. It fareth many times with men's opinions as with rumours and reports. "That which a credible person telleth is easily thought probable by such as are well persuaded of him. But if two, or three, or four, agree all in the same tale, they judge it then to be out of controversy, and so are many times overtaken for want of due consideration; either some common cause leading them all into error, or one man's oversight deceiving many through their too much credulity and easiness of belief." Though ten persons be brought to give testimony in any cause, yet if the knowledge they have of the thing whereunto they come as witnesses, appear to have grown from some one amongst them, and to have spread itself from hand to hand, they all are in force but as one testimony. Nor is it otherwise here where the daughter churches do speak their mother's dialect; here where so many sing one song, by reason that he is the guide of the choir, concerning whose deserved authority amongst even the gravest divines we have already spoken at large. Will ye ask what should move so many learned to be followers of one man's judgment, no necessity of argument forcing them thereunto? Your demand is answered by yourselves. Loth ye are to think that they, whom ye judge to have attained as sound knowledge in all points of doctrine as any since the Apostles' time, should mis-

[1] Galen. clas. 2, lib. de cujusque Anim. Peccat. Notitia atque Medela, t. i. p. 366. Basil. 1538.

take in discipline[1]. Such is naturally our affection, that whom in great things we mightily admire, in them we are not persuaded willingly that any thing should be amiss. The reason whereof is, "for that as dead flies putrify the ointment of the apothecary, so a little folly him that is in estimation for wisdom[2]." This in every profession hath too much authorized the judgments of a few. This with Germans hath caused Luther, and with many other churches Calvin, to prevail in all things. Yet are we not able to define, whether the wisdom of that God, who setteth before us in holy Scripture so many admirable patterns of virtue, and no one of them without somewhat noted wherein they were culpable; to the end, that "to Him alone it might always be acknowledged, "Thou only art holy, thou only art just;" might not permit those worthy vessels of his glory to be in some things blemished with the stain of human frailty, even for this cause, lest we should esteem of any man above that which behoveth.

V. Notwithstanding, as though ye were able to say a great deal more than hitherto your books have revealed to the world, earnest challengers ye are of trial by some public disputation. Wherein if the thing ye crave be no more than only leave to dispute openly about those matters that are in question, the schools in universities (for any thing I know) are open unto you. They have their yearly acts and commencements, besides other disputations both ordinary and upon occasion, wherein the several parts of our own ecclesiastical discipline are oftentimes offered unto that

[1] Petition to the Queen's Majesty, p. 14.
[2] Eccles. x. 1.

kind of examination; the learnedest of you have been
of late years noted seldom or never absent from thence
at the time of those greater assemblies; and the favour
of proposing there in convenient sort whatsoever ye
can object (which thing myself have known them to
grant of scholastical courtesy unto strangers) neither
hath (as I think) nor ever will (I presume) be denied
you.

If your suit be to have some great extraordinary
confluence, in expectation whereof the laws that already are should sleep and have no power over you,
till in the hearing of thousands ye all did acknowledge
your error and renounce the further prosecution of
your cause: haply they whose authority is required
unto the satisfying of your demand do think it both
dangerous to admit such concourse of divided minds,
and unmeet that laws, which being once solemnly
established are to exact obedience of all men and to
constrain thereunto, should so far stoop as to hold
themselves in suspense from taking any effect upon
you till some disputer can persuade you to be obedient.
A law is the deed of the whole body politic, whereof
if ye judge yourselves to be any part, then is the law
even your deed also. And were it reason in things of
this quality to give men audience, pleading for the
overthrow of that which their own very deed hath
ratified? Laws that have been approved may be (no
man doubteth) again repealed, and to that end also
disputed against, by the authors thereof themselves.
But this is when the whole doth deliberate what laws
each part shall observe, and not when a part refuseth
the laws which the whole hath orderly agreed upon.

Notwithstanding, forasmuch as the cause we main-

tain is (God be thanked) such as needeth not to shun
any trial, might it please them on whose approbation
the matter dependeth to condescend so far unto you
in this behalf, I wish heartily that proof were made
even by solemn conference in orderly and quiet sort,
whether you would yourselves be satisfied, or else
could by satisfying others draw them to your part.
Provided always, first, inasmuch as ye go about to
destroy a thing which is in force, and to draw in that
which hath not as yet been received; to impose on
us that which we think not ourselves bound unto,
and to overthrow those things whereof we are possessed; that therefore ye are not to claim in any such
conference other than the plaintiff's or opponent's
part, which must consist altogether in proof and con-
firmation of two things: the one, that our orders by
you condemned we ought to abolish; the other, that
yours we are bound to accept in the stead thereof:
secondly, because the questions in controversy between
us are many, if once we descend unto particularities;
that for the easier and more orderly proceeding therein
the most general be first discussed, nor any question
left off, nor in each question the prosecution of any
one argument given over and another taken in hand,
till the issue whereunto by replies and answers both
parts are come, be collected, read, and acknowledged
as well on the one side as on the other to be the plain
conclusion which they are grown into: thirdly, for
avoiding of the manifold inconveniences whereunto
ordinary and extemporal disputers are subject; as
also because, if ye should singly dispute one by one
as every man's own wit did best serve, it might be
conceived by the rest that haply some other would

have done more; the chiefest of you do all agree in
this action, that whom ye shall then choose your
speaker, by him that which is publickly brought into
disputation be acknowledged by all your consents
not to be his allegation but yours, such as ye all are
agreed upon, and have required him to deliver in all
your names; the true copy whereof being taken by a
notary, that a reasonable time be allowed for return
of answer unto you in the like form. Fourthly,
whereas a number of conferences have been had in
other causes with the less effectual success, by reason
of partial and untrue reports published afterwards
unto the world; that to prevent this evil, there be at
the first a solemn declaration made on both parts,
of their agreement to have that very book and no
other set abroad, wherein their present authorized
notaries do write those things fully and only, which
being written and there read, are by their own open
testimony acknowledged to be their own. Other
circumstances hereunto belonging, whether for the
choice of time, place, and language, or for prevention
of impertinent and needless speech, or to any end
and purpose else—they may be thought on when
occasion serveth.

In this sort to broach my private conceit for the
ordering of a public action I should be loth (albeit
I do it not otherwise than under correction of them
whose gravity and wisdom ought in such cases to
overrule,) but that so venturous boldness I see is a
thing now general; and am thereby of good hope, that
where all men are licensed to offend, no man will shew
himself a sharp accuser.

VI. What success God may give unto any such

kind of conference or disputation, we cannot tell. But of this we are right sure, that nature, Scripture, and experience itself, have all taught the world to seek for the ending of contentions by submitting itself unto some judicial and definitive sentence, whereunto neither part that contendeth may under any pretence or colour refuse to stand. This must needs be effectual and strong. As for other means without this, they seldom prevail. I would therefore know, whether for the ending of these irksome strifes, wherein you and your followers do stand thus formally divided against the authorized guides of this church, and the rest of the people subject unto their charge; whether I say ye be content to refer your cause to any other higher judgment than your own, or else intend to persist and proceed as ye have begun, till yourselves can be persuaded to condemn yourselves. If your determination be this, we can be but sorry that ye should deserve to be reckoned with such, of whom God himself pronounceth, "The way of peace they have not known[1]."

Ways of peaceable conclusion there are, but these two certain: the one, a sentence of judicial decision given by authority thereto appointed within ourselves; the other, the like kind of sentence given by a more universal authority. The former of which two ways God himself in the Law prescribeth, and his Spirit it was which directed the very first Christian churches in the world to use the latter.

The ordinance of God in the Law was this[2]. "If there arise a matter too hard for thee in judgment, between blood and blood, between plea, &c. then

---

[1] Rom. iii. 17.   [2] Deut. xvii. 8.

shalt thou arise, and go up unto the place which the Lord thy God shall choose; and thou shalt come unto the priests of the Levites, and unto the judge that shall be in those days, and ask, and they shall shew thee the sentence of judgment, and thou shalt do according to that thing, which they of that place which the Lord hath chosen shew thee, and thou shalt observe to do according to all that they inform thee; according to the law which they shall teach thee, and according to the judgment which they shall tell thee, shalt thou do; thou shalt not decline from the thing which they shall shew thee to the right hand nor to the left. And that man that will do presumptuously, not hearkening unto the priest (that standeth before the Lord thy God to minister there) or unto the judge, that man shall die, and thou shall take away evil from Israel."

When there grew in the Church of Christ a question, Whether the Gentiles believing might be saved, although they were not circumcised after the manner of Moses, nor did observe the rest of those legal rites and ceremonies whereunto the Jews were bound; after great dissension and disputation about it, their conclusion in the end was to have it determined by sentence at Jerusalem; which was accordingly done in a council there assembled for the same purpose[1]. Are ye able to allege any just and sufficient cause wherefore absolutely ye should not condescend in this controversy to have your judgments overruled by some such definitive sentence, whether it fall out to be given with or against you; that so these tedious contentions may cease?

Ye will perhaps make answer, that being persuaded

[1] Acts xv.

already as touching the truth of your cause, ye are not to hearken unto any sentence, no not though Angels should define otherwise, as the blessed Apostle's own example teacheth: again, that men, yea councils, may err; and that, unless the judgment given do satisfy your minds, unless it be such as ye can by no further argument oppugn, in a word, unless you perceive and acknowledge it yourselves consonant with God's word; to stand unto it not allowing it were to sin against your own consciences.

But consider I beseech you first as touching the Apostle, how that wherein he was so resolute and peremptory, our Lord Jesus Christ made manifest unto him even by intuitive revelation, wherein there was no possibility of error. That which you are persuaded of, ye have it no otherwise than by your own only probable collection, and therefore such bold asseverations as in him were admirable, should in your mouths but argue rashness. God was not ignorant that the priests and judges, whose sentence in matters of controversy he ordained should stand, both might and oftentimes would be deceived in their judgment. Howbeit, better it was in the eye of His understanding, that sometime an erroneous sentence definitive should prevail, till the same authority perceiving such oversight, might afterwards correct or reverse it, than that strifes should have respite to grow, and not come speedily unto some end.

Neither wish we that men should do any thing which in their hearts they are persuaded they ought not to do, but this persuasion ought (we say) to be fully settled in their hearts; that in litigious and controversed causes of such quality, the will of God is to have them do whatsoever the sentence of judicial and final decision shall determine, yea, though it seem in their private opinion to swerve utterly from that which is right: as no doubt many times the sentence amongst the Jews did seem unto one part or other contending, and yet in this case, God did then allow them to do that which in their private judgment it seemed, yea and perhaps truly seemed, that the law did disallow. For if God be not the author of confusion but of peace, then can he not be the author of our refusal, but of our contentment, to stand unto some definitive sentence; without which almost impossible it is that either we should avoid confusion, or ever hope to attain peace. To small purpose had the council of Jerusalem been assembled, if once their determination being set down, men might afterwards have defended their former opinions. When therefore they had given their definitive sentence, all controversy was at an end. Things were disputed before they came to be determined; men afterwards were not to dispute any longer, but to obey. The sentence of judgment finished their strife, which their disputes before judgment could not do. This was ground sufficient for any reasonable man's conscience to build the duty of obedience upon, whatsoever his own opinion were as touching the matter before in question. So full of wilfulness and self-liking is our nature, that without some definitive sentence, which being given may stand, and a necessity of silence on both sides afterward imposed, small hope there is that strifes thus far prosecuted will in short time quietly end.

Now it were in vain to ask you, whether ye could be content that the sentence of any court already erected should be so far authorized, as that among the Jews established by God himself, for the determining of all controversies: "That man which will do presumptuously, not hearkening unto the priest that standeth before the Lord to minister there, nor unto the judge, let him die." Ye have given us already to understand, what your opinion is in part concerning her sacred Majesty's court of high commission; the nature whereof is the same with that amongst the Jews, albeit the power be not so great. The other way happily may like you better, because Master Beza, in his last book save one[1] written about these matters, professeth himself to be now weary of such combats and encounters, whether by word or writing, inasmuch as he findeth that "controversies thereby are made but brawls;" and therefore wisheth "that in some common lawful assembly of churches all these strifes may at once be decided."

Shall there be in the meanwhile no "doings?" Yes. There are the weightier matters of the law, "judgment, and mercy, and fidelity[2]." These things we ought to do; and these things, while we contend about less, we leave undone. Happier are they whom the Lord when he cometh, shall find doing in these things, than disputing about "doctors, elders, and deacons." Or if there be no remedy but somewhat needs ye must do which may tend to the setting forward of your discipline; do that which wise men, who think some statute of the realm more fit to be repealed than to stand in force, are accustomed to do before they come to parliament where the place of enacting

---

[1] Præf. Tract. de Excom. et Presbyt.
[2] Matt. xxiii. 23.

is; that is to say, spend the time in re-examining more duly your cause, and in more thoroughly considering of that which ye labour to overthrow. As for the orders which are established, sith equity and reason, the law of nature, God and man, do all favour that which is in being, till orderly judgment of decision be given against it; it is but justice to exact of you, and perverseness in you it should be to deny, thereunto your willing obedience.

Not that I judge it a thing allowable for men to observe those laws which in their hearts they are steadfastly persuaded to be against the law of God: but your persuasion in this case ye are all bound for the time to suspend; and in otherwise doing, ye offend against God by troubling his Church without any just or necessary cause. Be it that there are some reasons inducing you to think hardly of our laws. Are those reasons demonstrative, are they necessary, or but mere probabilities only? An argument necessary and demonstrative is such, as being proposed unto any man and understood, the mind cannot choose but inwardly assent. Any one such reason dischargeth, I grant, the conscience, and setteth it at full liberty. For the public approbation given by the body of this whole church unto those things which are established, doth make it but probable that they are good. And therefore unto a necessary proof that they are not good it must give place. But if the skilfullest amongst you can shew that all the books ye have hitherto written be able to afford any one argument of this nature, let the instance be given. As for probabilities, what thing was there ever set down so agreeable with sound reason, but some probable show against it might be made? Is it meet that when publicly things are received, and have taken place, general obedience thereunto should cease to be exacted, in case this or that private person, led with some probable conceit, should make open protestation, "I Peter or John disallow them, and pronounce them nought?" In which case your answer will be, that concerning the laws of our church, they are not only condemned in the opinion of "a private man, but of thousands," yea and even "of those amongst which divers are in public charge and authority[1]." As though when public consent of the whole hath established any thing, every man's judgment being thereunto compared were not private, howsoever his calling be to some kind of public charge. So that of peace and quietness there is not any way possible, unless the probable voice of every entire society or body politic overrule all private of like nature in the same body. Which thing effectually proveth, that God, being author of peace and not of confusion in the Church, must needs be author of those men's peaceable resolutions, who concerning these things have determined with themselves to think and do as the church they are of decreeth, till they see necessary cause enforcing them to the contrary.

VII. Nor is mine own intent any other in these several books of discourse, than to make it appear unto you, that for the ecclesiastical laws of this land, we are led by great reason to observe them, and ye by no necessity bound to impugn them. It is no part of my secret meaning to draw you hereby into hatred, or to set upon the face of this cause any fairer

[1] T. C. lib. iii. p. 181.

glass than the naked truth doth afford; but my whole endeavour is to resolve the conscience, and to shew as near as I can what in this controversy the heart is to think, if it will follow the light of sound and sincere judgment, without either cloud of prejudice, or mist of passionate affection.

Wherefore seeing that laws and ordinances in particular, whether such as we observe, or such as yourselves would have established;—when the mind doth sift and examine them, it must needs have often recourse to a number of doubts and questions about the nature, kinds, and qualities of laws in general; whereof unless it be thoroughly informed, there will appear no certainty to stay our persuasion upon: I have for that cause set down in the first place an introduction on both sides needful to be considered: declaring therein what law is, how different kinds of laws there are, and what force they are of according unto each kind.

This done, because ye suppose the laws for which ye strive are found in Scripture, but those not against which ye strive; and upon this surmise are drawn to hold it as the very main pillar of your whole cause, "That Scripture ought to be the only rule of all our actions," and consequently that the church-orders which we observe being not commanded in Scripture, are offensive and displeasant unto God: I have spent the second Book in sifting of this point, which standeth with you for the first and chiefest principle whereon ye build.

Whereunto the next in degree is, That as God will have always a Church upon earth, while the world doth continue, and that Church stand in need of government; of which government it behoveth Himself to be both the Author and Teacher: so it cannot stand with duty that man should ever presume in any wise to change and alter the same; and therefore "that in Scripture there must of necessity be found some particular form of Polity Ecclesiastical, the Laws whereof admit not any kind of alteration."

The first three Books being thus ended, the fourth proceedeth from the general grounds and foundations of your cause unto your general accusations against us, as having in the orders of our church (for so you pretend) "corrupted the right form of church-polity with manifold popish rites and ceremonies, which certain reformed churches have banished from amongst them, and have thereby given us such example as" (you think) "we ought to follow." This your assertion hath herein drawn us to make search, whether these be just exceptions against the customs of our church, when ye plead that they are the same which the Church of Rome hath, or that they are not the same which some other reformed churches have devised.

Of those four Books which remain and are bestowed about the specialties of that cause which lieth in controversy, the first examineth the causes by you alleged, wherefore the public duties of Christian religion, as our prayers, our Sacraments, and the rest, should not be ordered in such sort as with us they are; nor that power, whereby the persons of men are consecrated unto the ministry, be disposed of in such manner as the laws of this church do allow. The second and third are concerning the power of jurisdiction: the one, whether laymen, such as your governing elders are, ought in all congregations for ever to be invested with that power; the other, whether bishops may have that power over other pastors, and therewithal that honour, which with us they have? And because besides the power of order which all consecrated persons have, and the power of jurisdiction which neither they all nor they only have, there is a third power, a power of ecclesiastical dominion, communicable, as we think, unto persons not ecclesiastical, and most fit to be restrained unto the Prince or Sovereign commander over the whole body politic: the eighth Book we have allotted unto this question, and have sifted therein your objections against those pre-eminences royal which thereunto appertain.

Thus have I laid before you the brief of these my travails, and presented unto your view the limbs of that cause litigious between us: the whole entire body whereof being thus compact, it shall be no troublesome thing for any man to find each particular controversy's resting-place, and the coherence it hath with those things, either on which it dependeth, or which depend on it.

VIII. The case so standing therefore, my brethren, as it doth, the wisdom of governors ye must not blame, in that they further also forecasting the manifold strange and dangerous innovations which are more than likely to follow if your discipline should take place, have for that cause thought it hitherto a part of their duty to withstand your endeavours that way. The rather, for that they have seen already some small beginnings of the fruits thereof, in them who concurring with you in judgment about the necessity of that discipline, have adventured without more ado to separate themselves from the rest of the Church, and to put your speculations in execution. These men's hastiness the warier sort of you doth not commend; ye wish they had held themselves longer in, and not so dangerously flown abroad before the feathers of the cause had been grown; their error with merciful terms ye reprove, naming them, in great commiseration of mind, your "poor brethren." They on the contrary side more bitterly accuse you as their "false brethren;" and against you they plead, saying: "From your breasts it is that we have sucked things, which when ye delivered unto us ye termed that heavenly, sincere, and wholesome milk of God's word[1], howsoever ye now abhor as poison that which the virtue thereof hath wrought and brought forth in us. You sometime our companions, guides and familiars, with whom we have had most sweet consultations[2], are now become our professed adversaries, because we think the statute-congregations in England to be no true Christian churches; because we have severed ourselves from them; and because without their leave and license that are in civil authority, we have secretly framed our own churches according to the platform of the word of God. For of that point between you and us there is no controversy. Alas! what would ye have us to do? At such time as ye were content to accept us in the number of your own, your teachings we heard, we read your writings: and though we would, yet able we are not to forget with what zeal ye have ever professed, that in the English congregations (for so many of them as be ordered according unto their own laws) the very public service of God is fraught as touching matter with heaps of intolerable pollutions,

[1] 1 Pet. ii. 2.   [2] Psalm lv. 13.

4—2

and as concerning form, borrowed from the shop of
Antichrist; hateful both ways in the eyes of the Most
Holy; the kind of their government by bishops and
archbishops antichristian; that discipline which Christ
hath 'essentially tied,' that is to say, so united unto
his Church, that we cannot account it really to be his
Church which hath not in it the same discipline, that
very discipline no less there despised, than in the
highest throne of Antichrist[1]; all such parts of the
word of God as do any way concern that discipline
no less unsoundly taught and interpreted by all
authorized English pastors, than by Antichrist's
factors themselves; at baptism crossing, at the supper
of the Lord kneeling, at both, a number of other the
most notorious badges of antichristian recognizance
usual. Being moved with these and the like your
effectual discourses, whereunto we gave most attentive
ear, till they entered even into our souls, and were
as fire within our bosoms; we thought we might hereof
be bold to conclude, that sith no such antichristian
synagogue may be accounted a true church of Christ,
you by accusing all congregations ordered according
to the laws of England as antichristian, did mean to
condemn those congregations, as not being any of them
worthy the name of a true Christian church. Ye tell
us now it is not your meaning. But what meant your
often threatenings of them, who professing themselves
the inhabitants of Mount Sion, were too loth to depart
wholly as they should out of Babylon? Whereat our
hearts being fearfully troubled, we durst not, we durst
not continue longer so near her confines, lest her
plagues might suddenly overtake us, before we did

[1] Pref. against Dr Bancr.

cease to be partakers with her sins: for so we could not choose but acknowledge with grief that we were, when, they doing evil, we by our presence in their assemblies seemed to like thereof, or at leastwise not so earnestly to dislike, as became men heartily zealous of God's glory. For adventuring to erect the discipline of Christ without the leave of the Christian magistrate, haply ye may condemn us as fools, in that we hazard thereby our estates and persons further than you which are that way more wise think necessary: but of any offence or sin therein committed against God, with what conscience can you accuse us, when your own positions are, that the things we observe should every of them be dearer unto us than ten thousand lives; that they are the peremptory commandments of God; that no mortal man can dispense with them, and that the magistrate grievously sinneth in not constraining thereunto? Will ye blame any man for doing that of his own accord, which all men should be compelled to do that are not willing of themselves? When God commandeth, shall we answer that we will obey, if so be Cæsar will grant us leave? Is discipline an ecclesiastical matter or a civil? If an ecclesiastical, it must of necessity belong to the duty of the minister. And the minister (you say) holdeth all his authority of doing whatsoever belongeth unto the spiritual charge of the house of God even immediately from God himself, without dependency upon any magistrate. Whereupon it followeth, as we suppose, that the hearts of the people being willing to be under the sceptre of Christ, the minister of God, into whose hands the Lord himself hath put that sceptre, is without all excuse if thereby he guide them not. Nor do we find that hitherto greatly ye have disliked these churches abroad, where the people with direction of their godly ministers have even against the will of the magistrate brought in either the doctrine or discipline of Jesus Christ. For which cause we must now think the very same thing of you, which our Saviour did sometime utter concerning false-hearted Scribes and Pharisees, 'they say, and do not[1].'" Thus the foolish Barrowist deriveth his schism by way of conclusion, as to him it seemeth, directly and plainly out of your principles. Him therefore we leave to be satisfied by you from whom he hath sprung.

And if such by your own acknowledgment be persons dangerous, although as yet the alterations which they have made are of small and tender growth; the changes likely to ensue throughout all states and vocations within this land, in case your desire should take place, must be thought upon.

First concerning the supreme power of the Highest, they are no small prerogatives, which now thereunto belonging the form of your discipline will constrain it to resign; as in the last book of this treatise we have shewed at large.

Again it may justly be feared whether our English nobility, when the matter came in trial, would contentedly suffer themselves to be always at the call, and to stand to the sentence of a number of mean persons assisted with the presence of their poor teacher, a man (as sometimes it happeneth) though better able to speak, yet little or no whit apter to judge, than the rest: from whom, be their dealings never so absurd, (unless it be by way of complaint to

[1] Matt. xxiii. 3.

a synod,) no appeal may be made unto any one of higher power, inasmuch as the order of your discipline admitteth no standing inequality of courts, no spiritual judge to have any ordinary superior on earth, but as many supremacies as there are parishes and several congregations.

Neither is it altogether without cause that so many do fear the overthrow of all learning as a threatened sequel of this your intended discipline. For if "the world's preservation" depend upon "the multitude of the wise[1];" and of that sort the number hereafter be not likely to wax over-great, "when" (that wherewith the son of Sirach professeth himself at the heart grieved) "men of understanding are" already so "little set by[2]:" how should their minds whom the love of so precious a jewel filleth with secret jealousy even in regard of the least things which may any way hinder the flourishing estate thereof, choose but misdoubt lest this discipline, which always you match with divine doctrine as her natural and true sister, be found unto all kinds of knowledge a step-mother; seeing that the greatest worldly hopes, which are proposed unto the chiefest kind of learning, ye seek utterly to extirpate as weeds, and have grounded your platform on such propositions as do after a sort undermine those most renowned habitations, where through the goodness of Almighty God all commendable arts and sciences are with exceeding great industry hitherto (and so may they for ever continue) studied, proceeded in, and professed? To charge you as purposely bent to the overthrow of that, wherein so many of you have attained no small perfection, were injurious. Only

[1] Sap. vi. 24.   [2] Ecclus. xxvi. 28.

therefore I wish that yourselves did well consider, how opposite certain of your positions are unto the state of collegiate societies, whereon the two universities consist. Those degrees which their statutes bind them to take are by your laws taken away; yourselves who have sought them ye so excuse, as that ye would have men to think ye judge them not allowable, but tolerable only, and to be borne with, for some help which ye find in them unto the furtherance of your purposes, till the corrupt estate of the Church may be better reformed. Your laws forbidding ecclesiastical persons utterly the exercise of civil power must needs deprive the heads and masters in the same colleges of all such authority as now they exercise, either at home, by punishing the faults of those, who not as children to their parents by the law of nature, but altogether by civil authority are subject unto them; or abroad by keeping courts amongst their tenants. Your laws making permanent inequality amongst ministers a thing repugnant to the word of God, enforce those colleges, the seniors whereof are all or any part of them ministers under the government of a master in the same vocation, to choose as oft as they meet together a new president. For if so ye judge it necessary to do in synods, for the avoiding of permanent inequality amongst ministers, the same cause must needs even in these collegiate assemblies enforce the like. Except peradventure ye mean to avoid all such absurdities, by dissolving those corporations, and by bringing the universities unto the form of the school of Geneva. Which thing men the rather are inclined to look for, inasmuch as the ministry, whereinto their founders with singular providence have by the same statutes appointed them necessarily to enter at a certain time, your laws bind them much more necessarily to forbear, till some parish abroad call for them.

Your opinion concerning the law civil is that the knowledge thereof might be spared, as a thing which this land doth not need[1]. Professors in that kind being few, ye are the bolder to spurn at them, and not to dissemble your minds as concerning their removal: in whose studies although myself have not much been conversant, nevertheless exceeding great cause I see there is to wish that thereunto more encouragement were given; as well for the singular treasures of wisdom therein contained, as also for the great use we have thereof, both in decision of certain kinds of causes arising daily within ourselves, and especially for commerce with nations abroad, whereunto that knowledge is most requisite. The reasons wherewith ye would persuade that Scripture is the only rule to frame all our actions by, are in every respect as effectual for proof that the same is the only law whereby to determine all our civil controversies. And then what doth let, but that as those men may have their desire, who frankly broach it already that the work of reformation will never be perfect, till the law of Jesus Christ be received alone; so pleaders and counsellors may bring their books of the common law, and bestow them as the students of curious and needless arts[2] did theirs in the Apostles' time? I leave them to scan how far those words of yours may reach, wherein ye declare that, whereas now many houses lie waste through

[1] Humb. Motion to the L. L. p. 50.
[2] Acts xix. 19.

inordinate suits of law, "this one thing will shew the excellency of discipline for the wealth of the realm, and quiet of subjects; that the Church is to censure such a party who is apparently troublesome and contentious, and without *reasonable cause* upon a mere will and stomach doth vex and molest his brother, and trouble the country[1]." For mine own part I do not see but that it might very well agree with your principles, if your discipline were fully planted, even to send out your writs of surcease unto all courts of England besides, for the most things handled in them.

A great deal further I might proceed and descend lower. But forasmuch as against all these and the like difficulties your answer is[2], that we ought to search what things are consonant to God's will, not which be most for our own ease; and therefore that your discipline being (for such is your error) the absolute commandment of Almighty God, it must be received although the world by receiving it should be clean turned upside down; herein lieth the greatest danger of all. For whereas the name of divine authority is used to countenance these things, which are not the commandments of God, but your own erroneous collections; on him ye must father whatsoever ye shall afterwards be led, either to do in withstanding the adversaries of your cause, or to think in maintenance of your doings. And what this may be, God doth know. In such kinds of error the mind once imagining itself to seek the execution of God's will, laboureth forthwith to remove both things and persons which any way hinder it from taking place; and in such cases if any strange or new thing seem requisite to be

[1] Humb. Motion, p. 74.   [2] Counterp. p. 108.

done, a strange and new opinion concerning the lawfulness thereof is withal received and broached under countenance of divine authority.

One example herein may serve for many, to shew that false opinions, touching the will of God to have things done, are wont to bring forth mighty and violent practices against the hinderances of them; and those practices new opinions more pernicious than the first, yea most extremely sometimes opposite to that which the first did seem to intend. Where the people took upon them the reformation of the Church by casting out popish superstition, they having received from their pastors a general instruction "that whatsoever the heavenly Father hath not planted must be rooted out[1]," proceeded in some foreign places so far that down went oratories and the very temples of God themselves. For as they chanced to take the compass of their commission stricter or larger, so their dealings were accordingly more or less moderate. Amongst others there sprang up presently one kind of men, with whose zeal and forwardness the rest being compared were thought to be marvellous cold and dull. These grounding themselves on rules more general; that whatsoever the law of Christ commandeth not, thereof Antichrist is the author: and that whatsoever Antichrist or his adherents did in the world, the true professors of Christ are to undo; found out many things more than others had done, the extirpation whereof was in their conceit as necessary as of any thing before removed. Hereupon they secretly made their doleful complaints every where as they went[2],

[1] Matt. xv. 13.
[2] Guy de Brés contre l'Erreur des Anabaptistes, p. 3.

that albeit the world did begin to profess some dislike
of that which was evil in the kingdom of darkness, yet
fruits worthy of a true repentance were not seen; and
that if men did repent as they ought, they must endeavour to purge the earth of all manner evil, to the
end there might follow a new world afterward, wherein righteousness only should dwell. Private repentance
they said must appear by every man's fashioning his
own life contrary unto the customs and orders of this
present world, both in greater things and in less. To
this purpose they had always in their mouths those
greater things, charity, faith, the true fear of God, the
cross, the mortification of the flesh[1]. All their ex-
hortations were to set light of the things in this world,
to count riches and honours vanity, and in token thereof
not only to seek neither, but if men were possessors
of both, even to cast away the one and resign the other,
that all men might see their unfeigned conversion
unto Christ[2]. They were solicitors of men to fasts[3],
to often meditations of heavenly things, and as it were
conferences in secret with God by prayers, not framed
according to the frozen manner of the world, but
expressing such fervent desires as might even force
God to hearken unto them. Where they found men
in diet, attire, furniture of house, or any other way,
observers of civility and decent order, such they re-
proved as being carnally and earthly minded. Every
word otherwise than severely and sadly uttered seemed
to pierce like a sword through them[4]. If any man were
pleasant, their manner was presently with deep sighs
to repeat those words of our Saviour Christ, "Woe

---

[1] Guy de Brés, op. cit. p. 4.   [2] P. 16.
[3] Pp. 118, 119.   [4] Pp. 116, 120.

be to you which now laugh, for ye shall lament[1]."
So great was their delight to be always in trouble, that
such as did quietly lead their lives, they judged of all
other men to be in most dangerous case. They so much
affected to cross the ordinary custom in every thing,
that when other men's use was to put on better attire,
they would be sure to shew themselves openly abroad
in worse: the ordinary names of the days in the week
they thought it a kind of profaneness to use, and
therefore accustomed themselves to make no other
distinction than by numbers, the First, Second,
Third day[2].

From this they proceeded unto public reformation,
first ecclesiastical, and then civil. Touching the former,
they boldly avouched that themselves only had the
truth, which thing upon peril of their lives they would
at all times defend; and that since the Apostles lived,
the same was never before in all points sincerely
taught[3]. Wherefore that things might again be
brought to that ancient integrity which Jesus Christ
by his word requireth, they began to control the ministers of the gospel for attributing so much force and
virtue unto the scriptures of God read, whereas the
truth was, that when the word is said to engender
faith in the heart, and to convert the soul of man, or
to work any such spiritual divine effect, these speeches
are not thereunto appliable as it is read or preached,
but as it is ingrafted in us by the power of the Holy
Ghost opening the eyes of our understanding, and so
revealing the mysteries of God, according to that
which Jeremy promised before should be, saying, "I
will put my law in their inward parts, and I will write

[1] Luke vi. 25.   [2] Guy de Brés, op. cit. p. 117.   [3] P. 40.

it in their hearts[1]." The Book of God they notwithstanding for the most part so admired, that other
disputation against their opinions than only by allegation of Scripture they would not hear; besides it they
thought no other writings in the world should be
studied; insomuch as one of their great prophets ex-
horting them to cast away all respects unto human
writings, so far to his motion they condescended, that
as many as had any books save the Holy Bible in
their custody, they brought and set them publickly on
fire[2]. When they and their Bibles were alone together,
what strange fantastical opinion soever at any time
entered into their heads, their use was to think the
Spirit taught it them. Their phrensies concerning
our Saviour's incarnation, the state of souls departed,
and such-like, are things needless to be rehearsed.
And forasmuch as they were of the same suite with
those of whom the Apostle speaketh, saying, "They
are still learning, but never attain to the knowledge
of truth[3]," it was no marvel to see them every day
broach some new thing, not heard of before. Which
restless levity they did interpret to be their growing
to spiritual perfection, and a proceeding from faith to
faith[4]. The differences amongst them grew by this
mean in a manner infinite, so that scarcely was there
found any one of them, the forge of whose brain was
not possessed with some special mystery. Whereupon,
although their mutual contentions[5] were most fiercely
prosecuted amongst themselves, yet when they came
to defend the cause common to them all against the
adversaries of their faction, they had ways to lick one

[1] Jer. xxxi. 33.　　　　[2] Guy de Brés, op. cit. p. 27.
[3] 2 Tim. iii. 7, p. 65.　　[4] P. 66.　　[5] P. 135.

another whole; the sounder in his own persuasion
excusing *the dear brethren*[1], which were not so far
enlightened, and professing a charitable hope of the
mercy of God towards them notwithstanding their
swerving from him in some things. Their own ministers
they highly magnified as men whose vocation was
from God[2]; the rest their manner was to term dis-
dainfully Scribes and Pharisees[3], to account their
calling a human creature, and to detain the people as
much as might be from hearing them. As touching
Sacraments[4], Baptism administered in the Church of
Rome they judged to be but an execrable mockery and
no baptism; both because the ministers thereof in the
Papacy are wicked idolaters, lewd persons, thieves
and murderers, cursed creatures, ignorant beasts;
and also for that to baptize is a proper action belonging
unto none but the Church of Christ, whereas Rome
is Antichrist's synagogue. The custom of using god-
fathers and godmothers at christenings they scorned[5].
Baptizing of infants, although confessed by themselves
to have been continued ever sithence the very Apostles'
own times, yet they altogether condemned; partly because sundry errors are of no less antiquity[6]; and
partly for that there is no commandment in the gospel
of Christ which saith, "Baptize infants[7];" but he
contrariwise in saying, "Go preach and baptize," doth
appoint that the minister of baptism shall in that
action first administer doctrine, and then baptism; as
also in saying, "Whosoever doth believe and is baptized," he appointeth that the party to whom baptism
is administered shall first believe and then be baptized;

[1] P. 25.   [2] P. 71.   [3] P. 124.   [4] P. 764.
[5] P. 748.   [6] P. 514.   [7] Pp. 722, 726, 688.

to the end that believing may go before this sacrament
in the receiver, no otherwise than preaching in the
giver; sith equally in both[1], the law of Christ declareth
not only what things are required, but also in what
order they are required. The Eucharist they received
(pretending our Lord and Saviour's example) after
supper; and for avoiding all those impieties which
have been grounded upon the mystical words of
Christ, "This is my body, this is my blood," they
thought it not safe to mention either body or blood
in that sacrament, but rather to abrogate both, and
to use no words but these, "Take, eat, declare the
death of our Lord: Drink, shew forth our Lord's
death[2]." In rites and ceremonies their profession was
hatred of all conformity with the Church of Rome: for
which cause they would rather endure any torment
than observe the solemn festivals which others did,
inasmuch as Antichrist (they said) was the first in-
ventor of them[3].

The pretended end of their civil reformation was
that Christ might have dominion over all; that all
crowns and sceptres might be thrown down at his
feet; that no other might reign over Christian men
but he, no regiment keep them in awe but his discipline, amongst them no sword at all be carried besides
his, the sword of spiritual excommunication. For this
cause they laboured with all their might in over-
turning the seats of magistracy[4], because Christ hath
said, "Kings of nations[5];" in abolishing the execution
of justice[6], because Christ hath said, "Resist not evil;"
in forbidding oaths, the necessary means of judicial

---

[1] Guy de Brés, op. cit. p. 518.   [2] P. 38.   [3] P. 122.
[4] P. 841.   [5] [Luke xxii. 25.]   [6] P. 833.

trial[1], because Christ hath said, "Swear not at all:" finally, in bringing in community of goods[2], because Christ by his Apostles hath given the world such example, to the end that men might excel one another not in wealth the pillar of secular authority, but in virtue.

These men at the first were only pitied in their error, and not much withstood by any; the great humility, zeal, and devotion, which appeared to be in them, was in all men's opinion a pledge of their harmless meaning. The hardest that men of sound understanding conceived of them was but this, "O quam honesta voluntate miseri errant! With how good a meaning these poor souls do evil[3]!" Luther made request unto Frederick duke of Saxony[4], that within his dominion they might be favourably dealt with and spared, for that (their error exempted) they seemed otherwise right good men. By means of which merciful toleration they gathered strength, much more than was safe for the state of the commonwealth wherein they lived. They had their secret corner-meetings and assemblies in the night, the people flocked unto them by thousands[5].

The means whereby they both allured and retained so great multitudes were most effectual: first, a wonderful show of zeal towards God, wherewith they seemed to be even rapt in every thing they spake: secondly, a hatred of sin, and a singular love of integrity, which men did think to be much more than ordinary in them, by reason of the custom which they had to fill the ears of the people with invectives against

[1] P. 849.   [2] P. 40.   [3] Lactant. de Justit. lib. v. c. 19
[4] P. 6.   [5] Pp. 4, 20, 41, 42.

their authorized guides, as well spiritual as civil: thirdly, the bountiful relief wherewith they eased the broken estate of such needy creatures, as were in that respect the more apt to be drawn away[1]: fourthly, a tender compassion which they were thought to take upon the miseries of the common sort, over whose heads their manner was even to pour down showers of tears, in complaining that no respect was had unto them, that their goods were devoured by wicked cormorants, their persons had in contempt, all liberty both temporal and spiritual taken from them[2], that it was high time for God now to hear their groans, and to send them deliverance: lastly, a cunning sleight which they had to stroke and smooth up the minds of their followers, as well by appropriating unto them all the favourable titles, the good words, and the gracious promises in Scripture; as also by casting the contrary always on the heads of such as were severed from that retinue. Whereupon the people's common acclamation unto such deceivers was, "These are verily the men of God, these are his true and sincere prophets[3]." If any such prophet or man of God did suffer by order of law condign and deserved punishment, were it for felony, rebellion, murder, or what else, the people, (so strangely were their hearts enchanted,) as though blessed Saint Stephen had been again martyred, did lament that God took away his most dear servants from them[4].

In all these things being fully persuaded, that what they did, it was obedience to the will of God, and that all men should do the like; there remained, after speculation, practice, whereby the whole world there-

[1] Guy de Brés, op. cit. p. 55. [2] Pp. 6, 7. [3] P. 7. [4] P. 27.

unto (if it were possible) might be framed. This they saw could not be done but with mighty opposition and resistance; against which to strengthen themselves, they secretly entered into league of association[1]. And peradventure considering, that although they were many, yet long wars would in time waste them out; they began to think whether it might not be that God would have them do, for their speedy and mighty increase, the same which sometime God's own chosen people, the people of Israel, did. Glad and fain they were to have it so; which very desire was itself apt to breed both an opinion of possibility, and a willingness to gather arguments of likelihood, that so God himself would have it. Nothing more clear unto their seeming, than that a new Jerusalem being often spoken of in Scripture, they undoubtedly were themselves that new Jerusalem, and the old did by way of a certain figurative resemblance signify what they should both be and do. Here they drew in a sea of matter, by applying all things unto their own company, which are any where spoken concerning divine favours and benefits bestowed upon the old commonwealth of Israel: concluding that as Israel was delivered out of Egypt, so they spiritually out of the Egypt of this world's servile thraldom unto sin and superstition; as Israel was to root out the idolatrous nations, and to plant instead of them a people which feared God; so the same Lord's good will and pleasure was now, that these new Israelites should, under the conduct of other Joshuas, Samsons, and Gideons, perform a work no less miraculous in casting out violently the wicked from the earth, and establishing the kingdom of

[1] P. 6.

Christ with perfect liberty: and therefore, as the cause why the children of Israel took unto one man many wives, might be lest the casualties of war should any way hinder the promise of God concerning their multitude from taking effect in them; so it was not unlike that for the necessary propagation of Christ's kingdom under the Gospel the Lord was content to allow as much.

Now whatsoever they did in such sort collect out of Scripture, when they came to justify or persuade it unto others, all was the heavenly Father's appointment, his commandment, his will and charge. Which thing is the very point, in regard whereof I have gathered this declaration. For my purpose herein is to show, that when the minds of men are once erroneously persuaded that it is the will of God to have those things done which they fancy, their opinions are as thorns in their sides, never suffering them to take rest till they have brought their speculations into practice. The lets and impediments of which practice their restless desire and study to remove leadeth them every day forth by the hand into other more dangerous opinions, sometimes quite and clean contrary to their first pretended meanings: so as what will grow out of such errors as go masked under the cloak of divine authority, impossible it is that ever the wit of man should imagine, till time have brought forth the fruits of them: for which cause it behoveth wisdom to fear the sequels thereof, even beyond all apparent cause of fear. These men, in whose mouths at the first sounded nothing but only mortification of the flesh, were come at the length to think they might lawfully have their six or seven wives apiece; they which at the first thought judgment and justice itself to be merciless cruelty, accounted at the length their own hands sanctified with being embrued in Christian blood; they who at the first were wont to beat down all dominion, and to urge against poor constables, "Kings of nations;" had at the length both consuls and kings of their own erection amongst themselves: finally, they which could not brook at the first that any man should seek, no not by law, the recovery of goods injuriously taken or withheld from him, were grown at the last to think they could not offer unto God more acceptable sacrifice, than by turning their adversaries clean out of house and home, and by enriching themselves with all kind of spoil and pillage; which thing being laid to their charge, they had in a readiness their answer[1], that now the time was come, when according to our Saviour's promise, "the meek ones must inherit the earth[2];" and that their title hereunto was the same which the righteous Israelites had unto the goods of the wicked Egyptians[3].

Wherefore sith the world hath had in these men so fresh experience, how dangerous such active errors are, it must not offend you though touching the sequel of your present mispersuasions much more be doubted, than your own intents and purposes do haply aim at. And yet your words already are somewhat, when ye affirm, that your Pastors, Doctors, Elders, and Deacons, ought to be in this Church of England, "whether her Majesty and our state will or no[4];" when for the animating of your confederates ye publish the musters which ye have made of your own bands, and proclaim

[1] Guy de Brés, op. cit. p. 41.   [2] Matt. v. 5.
[3] Exod. xi. 2.   [4] Mart. in his third Libel.

them to amount I know not to how many thousands; when ye threaten, that sith neither your suits to the parliament, nor supplications to our convocation-house, neither your defences by writing, nor challenges of disputation in behalf of that cause are able to prevail, we must blame ourselves, if to bring in discipline some such means hereafter be used as shall cause all our hearts to ache[1]. "That things doubtful are to be construed in the better part," is a principle not safe to be followed in matters concerning the public state of a commonweal. But howsoever these and the like speeches be accounted as arrows idly shot at random, without either eye had to any mark, or regard to their lighting-place; hath not your longing desire for the practice of your discipline brought the matter already unto this demurrer amongst you, whether the people and their godly pastors that way affected ought not to make separation from the rest, and to begin the exercise of discipline without the licence of civil powers, which licence they have sought for, and are not heard? Upon which question as ye have now divided yourselves, the warier sort of you taking the one part, and the forwarder in zeal the other; so in case these earnest ones should prevail, what other sequel can any wise man imagine but this, that having first resolved that attempts for discipline without superiors are lawful, it will follow in the next place to be disputed what may be attempted against superiors which will not have the sceptre of that discipline to rule over them? Yea even by you which have stayed yourselves from running headlong with the other sort, somewhat notwithstanding there hath been done with-

[1] Demonstr. in the Pref.

out the leave or liking of your lawful superiors, for the exercise of a part of your discipline amongst the clergy thereunto addicted. And lest examination of principal parties therein should bring those things to light, which might hinder and let your proceedings; behold, for a bar against that impediment, one opinion ye have newly added unto the rest even upon this occasion, an opinion to exempt you from taking oaths which may turn to the molestation of your brethren in that cause. The next neighbour opinion whereunto when occasion requireth may follow, for dispensation with oaths already taken, if they afterwards be found to import a necessity of detecting aught which may bring such good men into trouble or damage, whatsoever the cause be. O merciful God, what man's wit is there able to sound the depth of those dangerous and fearful evils, whereinto our weak and impotent nature is inclinable to sink itself, rather than to shew an acknowledgment of error in that which once we have unadvisedly taken upon us to defend, against the stream as it were of a contrary public resolution!

Wherefore if we any thing respect their error, who being persuaded even as you are have gone further upon that persuasion than you allow; if we regard the present state of the highest governor placed over us, if the quality and disposition of our nobles, if the orders and laws of our famous universities, if the profession of the civil or the practice of the common law amongst us, if the mischiefs whereinto even before our eyes so many others have fallen headlong from no less plausible and fair beginnings than yours are: there is in every of these considerations most just cause to fear lest our hastiness to embrace a thing of so perilous consequence should cause posterity to feel those evils, which as yet are more easy for us to prevent than they would be for them to remedy.

IX. The best and safest way for you therefore, my dear brethren, is, to call your deeds past to a new reckoning, to reexamine the cause ye have taken in hand, and to try it even point by point, argument by argument, with all the diligent exactness ye can; to lay aside the gall of that bitterness wherein your minds have hitherto over-abounded, and with meekness to search the truth. Think ye are men, deem it not impossible for you to err; sift unpartially your own hearts, whether it be force of reason or vehemency of affection, which hath bred and still doth feed these opinions in you. If truth do any where manifest itself, seek not to smother it with glosing delusions, acknowledge the greatness thereof, and think it your best victory when the same doth prevail over you.

That ye have been earnest in speaking or writing again and again the contrary way, shall be no blemish or discredit at all unto you. Amongst so many so huge volumes as the infinite pains of St. Augustine have brought forth, what one hath gotten him greater love, commendation and honour, than the book wherein he carefully collecteth his own oversights, and sincerely condemneth them? Many speeches there are of Job's whereby his wisdom and other virtues may appear; but the glory of an ingenuous mind he hath purchased by these words only, "Behold, I will lay mine hand on my mouth; I have spoken once, yet will I not therefore maintain argument; yea twice, howbeit for that cause further I will not proceed[1]."

[1] Job xl. 4, 5.

Far more comfort it were for us (so small is the joy we take in these strifes) to labour under the same yoke, as men that look for the same eternal reward of their labours, to be joined with you in bands of indissoluble love and amity, to live as if our persons being many our souls were but one, rather than in such dismembered sort to spend our few and wretched days in a tedious prosecuting of wearisome contentions: the end whereof, if they have not some speedy end, will be heavy even on both sides. Brought already we are even to that estate which Gregory Nazianzen mournfully describeth, saying[1], "My mind leadeth me" (sith there is no other remedy) "to fly and to convey myself into some corner out of sight, where I may scape from this cloudy tempest of maliciousness, whereby all parts are entered into a deadly war amongst themselves, and that little remnant of love which was, is now consumed to nothing. The only godliness we glory in, is to find out somewhat whereby we may judge others to be ungodly. Each other's faults we observe as matter of exprobration and not of grief. By these means we are grown hateful in the eyes of the heathens themselves, and (which woundeth us the more deeply) able we are not to deny but that we have deserved their hatred. With the better sort of our own our fame and credit is clean lost. The less we are to marvel if they judge vilely of us, who although we did well would hardly allow thereof. On our backs they also build that are lewd, and what we object one against another, the same they use to the utter scorn and disgrace of us all. This we have gained by our mutual home-dissensions. This we are worthily

[1] Greg. Naz. in Apol.

rewarded with, which are more forward to strive than becometh men of virtuous and mild disposition."

But our trust in the Almighty is, that with us contentions are now at their highest float, and that the day will come (for what cause of despair is there?) when the passions of former enmity being allayed, we shall with ten times redoubled tokens of our unfeignedly reconciled love, shew ourselves each towards other the same which Joseph and the brethren of Joseph were at the time of their interview in Egypt. Our comfortable expectation and most thirsty desire whereof what man soever amongst you shall any way help to satisfy, (as we truly hope there is no one amongst you but some way or other will,) the blessings of the God of peace, both in this world and in the world to come, be upon him moe than the stars of the firmament in number.